U.S. Department of Justice
National Institute of Corrections

BUILDING PARTNERSHIPS

A SYSTEMS APPROACH
TO

PARTNERSHIPS IN
CORRECTIONS

NATIONAL INSTITUTE OF CORRECTIONS
Morris L. Thigpen, Director

NIC Academy
Ida M. Halasz, Ph.D., Acting Chief

1960 Industrial Circle, Suite A
Longmont, Colorado 8050 1

Telephone: 303-682-0382
Toll Free: 800-995-6429
FTS:322-5000
FAX:3030682-0469
TDD:202-724-3156

Community Corrections Division
George Keiser, Chief
202-307-3995

Prisons Division
Susan M. Hunter, Chief
202-307-1300

Jails Division
Michael O'Toole, Chief
303-682-0639
800-995-6429

NATIONAL INSTITUTE OF CORRECTIONS ACADEMY
MISSION STATEMENT

The mission of the National Institute of Corrections Academy is to serve as a catalyst through training, technical assistance, and related services to enhance the leadership, professionalism, and effectiveness of correctional personnel in operating safe, efficient, humane and constitutional systems.

NIC ACADEMY
LESSON PLAN COVER SHEET

Course Title: **Building Partnerships " A Systems Approach"**

Lesson Title: **Defining Partnership in Corrections**

Instructor(s) **Experienced Correctional Trainers**

Prepared by **Vic Jacobsen**   Date **July 17, 1995**

Time Frame

   Total __3__ hrs., __30__ min.

   Suggested Schedule:

   Day: One

   Time(s):8:30 - 12:00 Noon

Target Population: Correctional Staff

Number of Participants 24

Space Requirement Large room with two breakout rooms

Performance Objectives

Following participation in the workshop participants will be able to:

1)   explain what a "partnership" is in their own words

2)   identify why partnerships are important

3)   generate a list of potential partnerships to meet agency program and operational needs

Evaluation Procedures

(How will objectives be evaluated?)

   Instructors evaluate the quality of the products developed by the participants and the quality of the surrounding discussions.

Methods/Techniques Lecture, Small Group Work Shops, Peer evaluation.

INSTRUCTOR MATERIALS	REFERENCES

INSTRUCTOR MATERIALS

Equipment and Supplies Needed

_X_ Flipchart & Stands   _2_ Number Needed

___ Chalkboard

___ 16mm Projector
Film Length: ___ min.

___ Slide Projector
Type: ___ Carousel
           ___ Tray
           ___ Sound-on-Slide

___ Screen

_X_ Flipchart Pads   _2_ Number Needed

_X_ Felt-Tip Markers _3_ Different Colors

_ Masking Tape (size 1/2") _2_ Rolls Needed

___ Other _____

REFERENCES

_ Videotape Player

Type: ___ 1/2" VHS
      ___ Other (Specify)

      ___ Videotape length: _ min.

___ Videotape recorder with camera

_ TV(s) ___ 23" ___ 27" ___ 33"
       (Indicate size & quantity)

__ VIDEOSHOW

_ Overhead Projector

___ Computer(s): Quan: 1 or 2

___ _____

Student Materials (Handouts)

Title*	#Needed From Academy	When Distributed	Comments

*Copyright clearances will need to be obtained, unless otherwise indicated

LESSON PLAN: Correctional Partnership Workshop

CONTENT	TRAINERS NOTES

I ANTICIPATORY SET

The final phase of this training requires that participants demonstrate the knowledge and skill they have obtained regarding correctional partnerships. One of the best ways to accomplish this is to have the participants apply the new knowledge to their own work environment.

To accomplish this each participant agency (if more than one participant is representing the same agency they may team up) shall go through the development steps identified in the curriculum as it relates to a back home project.

II GUIDED PRACTICE
INSTRUCTIONS

In small group, each jurisdiction, agency, department etc. develops a plan for using a correctional partnership to resolve a problem or enhance the present level of service.   To accomplish this each jurisdiction must respond to the following questions:

1)   Why do you believe your agency should form a partnership? (Needs Assessment)

2)   What partnership model will be formed and how will the partnership be organized?

3)   Who are the stakeholders, the nature of their stake, and their position (positive or negative)? Which of the stakeholders will be sought as partners and why?

4)   How, when and where will the partnership be implemented and how will it be supported?

5)   What evaluation strategies will be used to

HAND OUT ASSIGNMENT
SHEET OR WRITE ON
FLIP CHART

EXPLAIN THE
ASSIGNMENT

LESSON PLAN: Correctional Partnership Workshop

CONTENT	TRAINERS NOTES

determine the effectiveness of the partnership?

Planning Session
Participants are given 60-90 minutes to complete their assignment. Each jurisdiction must respond to each question in writing, preferably on flip chart paper. Instructor should monitor the progress of each jurisdiction. Encourage participants to share their ideas in the groups and to seek assistance from each other.

IDEALLY, THERE SHOULD -BE ONE INSTRUCTOR WITH EACH SMALL GROUP. HOWEVER, IT THIS IS NOT POSSIBLE, THE INSTRUCTOR(S) SHOULD CIRCULATE AMONG THE GROUPS.

Report Out
Upon expiration of the time limit (90 minutes) or completion of the task, which ever arrives first. Each participating jurisdiction should present their project to the small group and receive feedback. The use of flip charts is encouraged. Each jurisdiction is allotted 15 minutes of the group's time to present their product and receive feedback. Given a six person group, the report out should last a total of 90 minutes.-

INSTRUCTOR CONTINUES TO CIRCULATE

III CLOSEOUT/SUMMARY
Following the report outs the class should meet as a whole group for closeout, evaluation and graduation.

JURISDICTION ASSIGNMENT

Each jurisdiction has 90 minutes to prepare your response to the following questions. You final product should be on flip chart paper. Following the preparation period, each jurisdiction is allotted 15 minutes to present their product to the small group and receive feedback.

1) Why do you believe your agency should form a partnership? (Needs Assessment)

2) What partnership model will be formed and how will the partnership be organized?

3) Who are the stakeholders, the nature of their stake, and their position (positive or negative)? Which of the stakeholders will be sought as partners and why?

4) How, when and where will the partnership be implemented and how will it be supported?

5) What evaluation strategies will be used to determine the effectiveness of the partnership?

Methods/Techniques Lecture, Large Group Discussions, Video Tape, Small Group Work.

INSTRUCTOR MATERIALS Joel Barker Tape, "Discovering the Future"	**REFERENCES** Forging Community Partnerships, Patrick Wack, Research Assistant, APPA, Perspectives, Winter, 1995.

Equipment and Supplies Needed

_X_ Flipchart & Stands   _2_ Number Needed

___ Chalkboard

___ 16mm Projector
Film Length: ___ min.

___ Slide Projector
      Type: ___ Carousel
              ___ Tray
              ___ Sound-on-Slide

___ Screen

_X_ Flipchart Pads   _2_ Number Needed

_X_ Felt-Tip Markers   _3_ Different Colors

_ Masking Tape (size 1/2") _2_ Rolls Needed

___ Other _____

_X_ Videotape Player

   Type: _X_ 1/2" VHS
        ___ Other (Specify)

      ___ Videotape length: ___ min.

___ Videotape recorder with camera

_xx_ TV(s) ___ 23" ___ 27" ___ 33"
     (Indicate size & quantity)

___ VIDEOSHOW

_XX_ Overhead Projector

___ Computer(s): Quan: 1 or 2

___ _____

Student Materials (Handouts)			
Title*	#Needed From Academy	When Distributed	Comments

*Copyright clearances will need to be obtained, unless otherwise indicated

LESSON PLAN: Defining Partnerships

CONTENT	TRAINERS NOTES

I. Anticipatory Set

SHOW OVERHEAD # 1
Defining Partnerships

A) OBJECTIVES
We are going to begin our discussion of partnerships by attempting to frame exactly what we mean when we use the term partnership. The specific performance objectives of this session are:

Following participation in the workshop participants will be able to:

SHOW OVERHEAD #2
Performance Objectives...

1) explain what a "partnership" is in their own words

2) identify why partnerships are important

3) generate a list of potential partnerships to meet agency program and operational needs

B) STATISTICS
The idea of partnership has become a very popular subject of discussion in the field of corrections. In recent years, partnerships are forming for a variety of reasons, not the least of which is the failure of the criminal justice system to deal with crime and punishment. The following statistics, were published in the Winter 1995 issue of Perspectives illustrates this point:

SHOW OVERHEAD #3
STATISTICS

the United States spent $25 billion on corrections in 1992 with state and local governments paying most of the amount (Edna McConnell Clark Foundation, [EMCF 1993])

The United States has the highest rate of incarceration of any other industrialized nation (EMCF 1993)

in 1992, nearly one third of all jails in the country were under court order to reduce crowding or improve conditions (EMCF 1993)

SHOW OVERHEAD #4

LESSON PLAN: Defining Partnerships

CONTENT	TRAINERS NOTES

this has contributed to the fact that over 2 million adults are on probation and over half-million are on parole (Bureau of Justice Statistics, 1994).

These frightening statistics are an indication that we in the field of corrections do not have the answers and its time for us to look far beyond our criminal justice system for solutions.   The ability of corrections professionals to seek answers from persons outside the criminal justice family is tempered by their willingness to involve others. It is also dependent on our willingness to promote and accept change.

C) VIDEO TAPE
To illustrate this point I am going to show a video tape. This tape illustrates how some of the most impressive technological changes have occurred because of the involvement of persons outside the profession where the changes were needed; As you watch the film pay particular attention to the involvement of stakeholders outside the profession or organization involved.

Note: Show the Barker tape depicting the impact of change. The tape runs about 30 minutes. At the end of the tape conduct a group discussion regarding the initiation
of change in the criminal justice system. Break into small groups and ask each group to cite examples of changes that have occurred the field over the past decade and who or what group initiated the changes. (Samples: privatization, electronic monitoring, increased use of computers and information, direct supervision, intense supervision, classification etc). After compiling the list have each group give you an item from their list and record them on a flip chart. Continue from group to group until the lists are exhausted or you feel you have a good list to work with. Now go back over the list and ask the group to

LESSON PLAN: Defining Partnerships

CONTENT	TRAINERS NOTES

identify who or what it was that initiated the changes cited.

IF THE JOEL BARKER TAPE IS NOT IN YOUR VIDEO LIBRARY YOU MAY SELECT ANOTHER TAPE THAT DEPICTS HOW THE FUTURE OF ORGANIZATIONS' TO A GREAT EXTENT ARE INFLUENCED BY THOSE OUTSIDE THE ORGANIZATION

This exercise demonstrates the influence people and organizations outside of corrections have on our everyday work. It sets the stage for why we should seek partnerships with persons and organizations outside corrections.

Given this background why do you think it is important for us (corrections professionals) to form partnerships?

II INPUT

A) PARTNERSHIP
Given the examples of how change occurs, it seems that if the corrections profession is truly seeking resolution, it must look outside the field for assistance. Hence the idea of partnerships. The field of corrections must seek partnerships with other disciplines, professions, organizations, groups and people if it is to better respond to the needs of the community.

We are using this term Partnership rather loosely. When I use the term partnership, what does it mean to you?

Note: Solicit examples and/or definitions of what the word partnership means to the participants. Record the ideas on the flip chart, briefly discussing each. At the conclusion of the discussions close out the thought by sharing the following definition of partners and partnerships taken from Webster's Dictionary.

LESSON PLAN: Defining Partnerships

CONTENT	TRAINERS NOTES

Partners are people associated in a common undertaking and sharing risks and profits.

Partnerships are an association of persons who share risks and profits in a business or other joint venture.

I I I Guided Practice.

A) TYPES OF PARTNERSHIPS
Given our experience up this point, it is becoming clearer just how the field of corrections may benefit by forming partnerships with a variety of entities. 'In fact in some agencies this is already occurring throughout the country. Lets take a few minutes to identify existing partnership that have been organized and analyze how each of the partners shares in the risks and profits of the partnership.

First lets take a few minutes to identify the various kinds of partnerships that exist within the field.

Conduct a very brief group discussion around the following questions. Just make sure that the participants have a good handle on the nature and kinds of partnerships that exist in the field of corrections i.e., volunteer programs, private sector programs, advisory boards, mentors, education, training etc.

SHOW OVERHEAD #4
GROUP INSTRUCTIONS...

"Can you cite a few examples of correctional partnerships that exist today?"

B) GROUP EXERCISE
Following this brief five minute discussion break the large group up into 3-5 small groups. Arrange the groups around something that they have in common i.e. prisons, jails, community corrections, state agencies, local agencies. The primary objective is to have people with similar professional interests and experiences in the same group. Once the groups are organized give the following assignment.

LESSON PLAN: Defining Partnerships

CONTENT	TRAINERS NOTES

Group assignment:

1) In small groups identify at least one example of a correctional partnership that you believe is innovative and deserving of recognition.

2) On a flip chart page display the following:

     -name of the partnership
     -a graphic(picture) that depicts the nature of the partnership
     -names of the partners
     -the common goal shared by the partners
     -list examples of risks the partners share
     examples-
          failure
          loss of funds invested
          trusting operation to outsider
          negative feedback
          peer criticism
          staff resistance
     -list examples of profits or benefits shared by .
     the partners
     examples-
          monetary gain
          safer community
          reduced recidivism
          increased enrollment
          increased service

3) Be prepared, as a group, to present your product at the end of the preparation period (20 minutes).

Give the groups approximately 20-30 minutes to complete this task. Ensure that each group has sufficient markers and flip chart paper to complete the task. Upon completion have each group tape their product on the wall of the large classroom and present it to the rest of the group. Allow 20-30 minutes (5-10 minutes each) for the presentations and discussion of the group products.

LESSON PLAN: Defining Partnerships

CONTENT	TRAINERS NOTES

IV Summary

During the last couple of hours we have studied, at length, the nature and existence of partnerships in corrections. This experience has led us to better understand the value of partnerships, the structure of partnerships and the necessity of partnerships.

The modules to follow will assist us in knowing when and how to foster the development of partnerships.

Defining
Partnerships

Performance Objectives

Following participation in the workshop participants will be able to:

1)explain what a "partnership" is in their own words

2) identify why partnerships are important

3)generate a list of potential partnerships to meet agency program and operational needs

The following statistics, were published in the Winter 1995 issue of Perspectives illustrates this point:

the United States spent $25 billion on corrections in 1992 with state and local governments paying most of the amount (Edna McConnell Clark Foundation, [EMCF 1993])

The United States has the highest rate of incarceration of any other industrialized nation (EMCF 1993)

In 1992, nearly one third of all jails in the country were under court order to reduce crowding or improve conditions (EMCF 1993)

This has contributed to the fact that over 2 million adults are on probation and over half-million are on parole (Bureau of Justice Statistics, 1994).

NIC ACADEMY
LESSON PLAN COVER SHEET

Course Title: <u>Building Partnerships " A Systems Approach"</u>
Lesson Title: <u>Partnership Planning and Development, Part 1</u>
Instructor(s) <u>Experienced Correctional Trainers</u>
Prepared by <u>Vic Jacobsen</u>   Date <u>July 17, 1995</u>

Time Frame	Target Population: Correctional Staff

Total __4 hrs., _30_ min.
 	
Suggested Schedule:
 	
  Day: One
 	
  Time(s):1:00 - 4:30 P.M.
	Number of Participants 24
	
	Space Requirement Large room with two breakout rooms

Performance Objectives	Evaluation Procedures
Following participation in the workshop participants will be able to: 1) illustrate why building partnerships are important to the field of corrections 2) identify the six steps in developing a correctional partnership 3) develop strategies to enhance communication with the public, staff and administration 4) identify stakeholders both internal and external to the organization 5) analyze the role of stakeholders in developing and maintaining partnerships	(How will objectives be evaluated?) Instructors evaluate the quality of the products developed by the participants and the quality of the surrounding discussions.

Methods/Techniques Lecture, Large Group Discussions, Video Tape, Small Group Work.

INSTRUCTOR MATERIALS	REFERENCES <u>Interagency Agreement: A Rational Response to Irrational System</u>, John A. Lacour, Exceptional Children Developing Effective Coalitions: An Eight Step Guide, Larry Cohen, Nancy Baer, and Pam Satterwhite, Contra Costa County Health Services Department Prevention Program, 1991.)

Equipment and Supplies Needed
 	
 _X_ Flipchart & Stands _2_ Number Needed
 	
 ___ Chalkboard
 	
 ___ 16mm Projector
 Film Length: ___ min.
 	
 ___ Slide Projector
      Type: ___ Carousel
         ___ Tray
         ___ Sound-on-Slide
 ___ Screen
 	
 _X_ Flipchart Pads _2_ Number Needed
 	
 _X_ Felt-Tip Markers _3_ Different Colors
 	
 _ Masking Tape (size 1/2") _2_ Rolls Needed
 	
 ___ Other _____
	___ Videotape Player
	
	 Type: ___ 1/2" VHS
	     ___ Other (Specify)
	
	     ___ Videotape length: __ min.
	
	 ___ Videotape recorder with camera
	
	 _ TV(s) ___ 23" ___ 27" ___ 33"
	    (Indicate size & quantity)
	
	 ___ VIDEOSHOW
	
	 _ Overhead Projector
	
	 ___ Computer(s): Quan: 1 or 2
	
	 ___ _____

Student Materials (Handouts)			
Title*	#Needed From Academy	When Distributed	Comments

*Copyright clearances will need to be obtained, unless otherwise indicated

LESSON PLAN: Planning and Developing Partnerships, Part 1

CONTENT	TRAINERS NOTES

1. Anticipatory Set (60 Minutes)

Growth of Community Involvement

SHOW OVERHEAD #1
PLANNING AND
DEVELOPING
PARTNERSHIPS

Over the last decade the criminal justice community has realized the benefits of encouraging community involvement in crime prevention and neighborhood safety. Programs such as "Neighborhood Watch," "Weed and Seed" and "D.A.R.E." have proved successful deterrents to crime, drug trafficking and use. As often happens, the field of corrections is now evaluating the value of community involvement in secure and community based correctional programming.

Correctional agencies have been open to using community volunteers for at least two decades. Partnerships with colleges and universities for research and student intern placement are common. However, actually reaching out to the community, the business world, service organizations and support agencies to help with general or specific advice, assistance or service are far less common.

Following participation in the workshop participants will be able to:

OVERHEAD # 2
PERFORMANCE
OBJECTIVES. . .

    1) illustrate why building partnerships are important to the field of corrections

    2) identify the six steps in developing a correctional partnership

    3) develop strategies to enhance communication with the public, staff and administration

    4) identify stakeholders both internal and external to the organization

LESSON PLAN: Planning and Developing Partnerships, Part 1

CONTENT	TRAINERS NOTES

5) analyze the role of stakeholders in developing and maintaining partnerships

Why? To improve service. Several surveys now confirm that improving service is the highest priority of executives across America and Europe. A Gallup poll commissioned by the American Society for Quality Control found service quality the single most important issue in 615 companies. The Strategic Marketing Institute found the top three concerns of European corporations are:

(1) "coping with the increasing importance of product quality and greater service content,"

OVERHEAD # 3
TOP THREE CONCERNS

(2) "assessing changing customer characteristics," and

(3) "creating a marketing culture throughout the corporation."

Current drives for forming partnerships:

1. Concern about conserving and better using all types of resources

OVERHEAD #4
CURRENT DRIVES . . .

2. Tension and concerns about better use of the dollar.

3. The increasingly complex world we live in.

4. Increasingly rapid and complex change of values.

5. More people concerned about social-cause and quality of life.

LESSON PLAN: Planning and Development, Part 1

CONTENT	TRAINERS NOTES

6. Documented very productive experiences from previous collaborative activities.

Examples of successful partnerships:

OVERHEAD #5
SUCCESSFUL
PARTNERSHIPS. . .

Discouraging drug dealers in Cleveland, Ohio
A community based organization helped police remove drug pushers operating on a vacant lot. City officials then pitched in to help the nonprofit group build affordable, owner-occupied homes on the site.

Campaigning against youth violence in Minnesota
The Minnesota Crime Prevention Officers Association enlisted the support of families, public officials, and 45 statewide and local organizations, including schools and churches, to wage a campaign against youth violence.

Encouraging business participation in correctional industry programs, Washoe County Nevada
The jail industry advisory board helps with guiding the growth and development of the jail industry enterprises. Meeting quarterly the Board advises the Sheriff's Department on ways to employ and train more inmates while benefiting the citizens and businesses in the county. Similar boards operate on the state and federal level.

OVERHEAD #5
SUCCESSFUL
PARTNERSHIPS. . .

Neighborhood group consulted in the use of jail space, Hennepin County, MN
A neighborhood organization meets with correctional facility management on a regular basis to review the use of jail space and inmate classification. As the neighborhood and the facility are close to each other, this networking results in the residents feeling comfortable about the risk they take by living close to the facility.

LESSON PLAN: Planning and Developing Partnerships, Part 1

CONTENT	TRAINERS NOTES

Benefits of Partnerships:

1. Overlaps (duplication of services) are decreased

2. New connections are made   **OVERHEAD # 6 BENEFITS. . .**

3. More influence and power

4. Much more creativity

5. Reinforcing excitement

6. Attracts a needed variety of heads and hands

7. Creative questioning of traditional ways

8. Support for change and risk taking

(Source: Interagency Agreement: A Rational Response to Irrational System, John A. Lacour, Exceptional Children

Some traps in partnerships:

1. Fear of merger - loss of identity

2. Compromise means giving up turf and territory   **OVERHEAD # 7 SOME TRAPS. . .**

3. Fear of loss of control

4. Not enough time to keep people informed and involved

5. Documentation requirement

6. Inadequate resources

CONTENT	TRAINERS NOTES

2. Input

Introduction to the Development Process (30 minutes)

The research available in the" field of partnership development suggests that the method employed to form and operate a partnership is as important as the partnership itself. A wide variety of models are cited in publications by the Bureau of Justice Assistance, American Probation and Parole Association, National Institute of Corrections and a variety of individual authors and organizations. Each publication stresses the value of involving persons outside the agency or organization in solving problems and creating new paradigms,

The advancement of technology makes it easy for corrections officials to communicate with systems outside the norm. Corrections need not be isolated, but rather seen as an integral part of the community. Those persons or organizations that corrections officials have feared interference from the most, may well be our most valuable allies in the future. Seeking input and coordination from a variety of sources to better serve correctional clients makes sense.

Partnership Development Process

1. Needs Assessment - Why do we need help?

2. Model Identification - How should the partnership be organized?

3. Membership Recruitment - Who are our partners?

4. Start-up - How to get organized.

5. Maintenance - How to support the partnership.

6. Evaluation - How is the partnership doing?

OVERHEAD # 8
PARTNERSHIP
DEVELOPMENT
PROCESS. . .

LESSON PLAN: Planning and Development

CONTENT	TRAINERS NOTES

Step 1. Needs Assessment (60 Minutes)

Partnerships should not be created merely because they are popular. Staff must take great care to insure that any partnership formed responds to a need or accomplishes specific desirable outcomes. Needs assessments need not be strict statistical research, but can be more informal. Needs assessment is a process that helps us identify problems, unresolved issues, unmet needs, desires of our constituencies.

Residents or members of the community should help to identify the problems that exist or threaten to establish themselves. Facts and opinions should be assembled, with discussion incorporating everyone's concerns and culminating in consensus on several approaches toward resolution.

OVERHEAD #9
NEEDS ASSESSMENT

Exercise: guided practice
Ask the participants to break into four small groups. Their assignment is to "identify and describe three to five methods they can use to conduct a needs assessment for their agency, program, office or department." Methods should be listed and described on flip chart paper for posting. Each group should select a spokesperson to present their product to the large group. Allow 15-20 minutes for small group work and 30 minutes for report outs.

BREAK INTO SMALL
GROUPS. MONITOR
GROUP PROGRESS.
FACILITATE GROUP
REPORT OUT.

Example methods of determining needs
      survey the constituency (inmates, clients)
      survey the community residents
      survey community leaders
      survey other agencies
      survey staff
      conduct statistical analysis
      meet legislative mandate
      review evaluation data
      review annual reports
      review court cases

OVERHEAD #10
EXAMPLES OF NEEDS
ASSESSMENT

LESSON PLAN: Planning and Developing Partnerships, Part 1

CONTENT   TRAINERS NOTES

Step 2. Model Identification (50 minutes)

Partnerships can be organized in a variety of ways. However, all seek to improve services by increasing input and involvement in the criminal justice environment. The outcome of the needs assessment will dictate what kind of partnership your agency may benefit from A few examples of typical partnerships are:

Commissions -
    appointed by official bodies and usually consist of citizens rather than organizations. Commissions can be temporary bodies formed to address specific problems or issues.

Task Forces -
    accomplish a specific series of activities, often at the request of an overseeing body.   Task forces traditionally have a specific objective and once it is accomplished the task . force is disbanded.

OVERHEAD #11
MODELS . . .

Networks -
    imply communication and are generally loose-knit.   Strategy used by individuals and organizations to remain informed. Networks share information regularly and can be permanent or temporary.

Advisory Boards -
    provide suggestions and assistance to organizations or programs. Advisory boards are permanent bodies with changing memberships.

Consortia/Alliances -
    semi-official affiliation of organizations. Consortia normally the more structured of the two. Alliances and Consortia share resources

LESSON PLAN: Planning and Developing Partnerships, Part 1

CONTENT	TRAINERS NOTES

to better serve their constituency.

Coalitions -
serve to mobilize individuals or groups around a common program and generate power. May be long-term shifting or relatively permanent. Coalitions take a stand on issues and promote them.

OVERHEAD #12
CONSORTIA/ALLIANCES.

Inter-agency Agreement -
two or more organizations contract to support each other in their specific missions. Often the strengths of one organization are used to benefit another.

Contracts -
organizations contract with persons or organizations to provide service. Contracts have specific objectives and a time frame in which to accomplish them. Clearly delineate each parties responsibilities.

(Source: Developing Effective Coalitions: An Eight Step Guide, Larry Cohen, Nancy Baer, and Pam Satterwhite, Contra Costa County Health Services Department Prevention Program, 1991.)

Exercise: guided practice
In large group describe and discuss each model and ask the participants to cite specific examples of how the models have been applied in their organizations or fields. Create a flip chart for each listing the citations described by the group. Following the posting of the examples ask the group to identify others that are not listed that they believe are effective partnerships.

III GUIDED PRACTICE

(See exercises in INPUT)

IV CLOSING SUMMARY

FACILITATE GROUP
DISCUSSION. WRITE
EXAMPLES OF
PARTNERSHIPS ON FLIP
CHART.

LESSON PLAN: Planning and Developing Partnerships, Part 1

CONTENT	TRAINERS NOTES

Today we introduced the concept of partnerships in corrections. We identified the steps in forming partnerships and began working through each of the steps. We have discussed and cited examples of needs assessments and partnerships models.

In each group, take a few moments to evaluate the day. Discuss and record your evaluation of the day. Specifically, we request you give the instructors feedback in the areas of content (what was taught), methods (how it was taught), instructors (who taught the classes) and miscellaneous (facilities, environment, lodging etc.)

Select a spokesperson from your group to meet with the instructors for a ten minute closeout meeting. Take five minutes for your discussions and then the group is free to go. The spokesperson to meet with the instructors at (time and place).

PLANNING AND DEVELOPING PARTNERSHIPS

Performance Objectives
Following participation in the workshop participants will be able to:

1) illustrate why building partnerships are important to the field of corrections

2) identify the six steps in developing a correctional partnership

3) develop strategies to enhance communication with the public staff and administration

4) identify stakeholders both internal and external to the organization

5) analyze the role of stakeholders in developing and maintaining partnerships

The Strategic Marketing Institute found the top three concerns of European corporations are:

(1) "coping with the increasing importance of product quality and greater service content,"

(2) "assessing changing customer characteristics," and

(3) "creating a marketing culture throughout the corporation."

Current drives for forming partnerships:

1. Concern about conserving and better using all types of resources

2. Tension and concerns about better use of the dollar

3. The increasingly complex world we live in.

4. Increasingly rapid and complex change of values.

5. More people concerned about social-cause and quality of life.

6. Documented very productive experiences from previous collaborative activities.

Examples of successful partnerships:

Discouraging drug dealers in
Cleveland, Ohio

Campaigning against youth violence in
Minnesota

Encouraging business participation in
correctional industry programs!
Washoe County Nevada

Neighborhood group consulted in the
use of jail space, Hennepin County, MN

Benefits of Partnerships:

1. Overlaps (duplication of services) are decreased

2. New connections are made

3. More influence and power

4. Much more creativity

5. Reinforcing excitement

6. Attracts a needed variety of heads and hands

7. Creative questioning of traditional ways

8. Support for change and risk taking

Some traps in partnerships:

1. Fear of merger - loss of identity

2. Compromise means giving up turf and territory

3. Fear of loss of control

4. Not enough time to keep people informed and involved

5. Documentation requirement

6. Inadequate resources

Partnership Development Process

1. Needs Assessment - Why do we need help?

2. Model Identification - How should the partnership be organized?

3. Membership Recruitment - Who are our partners?

4. Start-up - How to get organized.

5. Maintenance - How to support the partnership.

6. Evaluation - How is the partnership doing?

NEEDS ASSESSMENT

Example methods of determining needs

survey the constituency (inmates, clients)
survey the community residents
survey community leaders
survey other agencies
survey staff
conduct statistical analysis
meet legislative mandate
review evaluation data
review annual reports
review court cases

A few examples of typical partnerships are:

Commissions -
appointed by official bodies and usually consist of citizens rather than organizations.

Task Forces -
accomplish a specific series of activities, often at the request of an overseeing body.-

Networks -
imply communication and are generally loose-knit.

Advisory Boards -
provide suggestions and assistance to organizations or programs.

Partnerships Cont'd

Consortia/Alliances -
  semi-official affiliation of
  organizations.

Coalitions -
  serve to mobilize individuals or
  groups around a common program
  and generate power.

Inter-agency Agreement -
  two or more organizations contract
  to support each other in their
  specific missions.

Contracts -
  organizations contract with persons
  or organizations to provide service.

LESSON PLAN COVER SHEET

Course Title: <u>Building Partnerships " A Systems Approach"</u>
Lesson Title: <u>Partnership Planning and Development, Part 2</u>
Instructor(s) <u>Experienced Correctional Trainers</u>
Prepared by <u>Vic Jacobsen</u> Date <u>July 17, 1995</u>

Time Frame	Target Population: Correctional Staff
Total <u>3</u> hrs., <u>30</u> min.	Number of Participants 24
Suggested Schedule:	
Day: Two	Space Requirement Large room with two breakout rooms
Time(s):8:30 - 12.00 Noon.	

Performance Objectives	Evaluation Procedures
Following participation in the workshop participants will be able to:	(How will objectives be evaluated?)
1) identify stakeholders both internal and external to the organization	Instructors evaluate the quality of the products developed by the participants and the quality of the surrounding discussions.
2) analyze the role of stakeholders in developing and maintaining partnerships	
3) identify stakeholders that are potential partners	
3) identify strategies for partnership startup, maintenance, and evaluation.	

Methods/Techniques Lecture, Large Group Discussions, Small Group Work.

INSTRUCTOR MATERIALS	REFERENCES Interagency Agreement: A Rational Response to Irrational System, John A. Lacour, Exceptional Children Developing Effective Coalitions: An Eight Step Guide, Larry Cohen, Nancy Baer, and Pam Satterwhite, Contra Costa County Health Services Department Prevention Program, 1991.)

Equipment and Supplies Needed

_X_ Flipchart & Stands   _2_ Number Needed

___ Chalkboard

___ 16mm Projector
Film Length: ___ min.

___ Slide Projector
    Type: ___ Carousel
             ___ Tray
             ___ Sound-on-Slide

___ Screen

_X_ Flipchart Pads   _2_ Number Needed

_X_ Felt-Tip Markers   _3_ Different Colors

_ Masking Tape (size 1/2") _2_ Rolls Needed

___ Other _____

___ Videotape Player

    Type: ___ 1/2" VHS
          ___ Other (Specify)

        ___ Videotape length: __ min.

___ Videotape recorder with camera

_ TV(s) ___ 23" ___ 27" ___ 33"
    (Indicate size & quantity)

___ VIDEOSHOW

_ Overhead Projector

·___ Computer(s): Quan: 1 or 2

___ _____

Student Materials (Handouts)

Title*	#Needed From Academy	When Distributed	Comments

*Copyright clearances will need to be obtained, unless otherwise indicated

LESSON PLAN: Planning and Developing Partnerships, Part 2

CONTENT	TRAINERS NOTES

Planning and Developing Partnerships (Continued)

I. ANTICIPATORY SET

(Discuss yesterday's feedback with the group, Discuss any changes.)

Yesterday, we introduced the concept of partnerships and worked through the first two steps of forming partnerships; Needs Assessment and Model Identification. Today we will continue this process by discussing Membership Recruitment, Start-up, Maintenance and Evaluation. Each step is crucial to the success of partnerships.

We will continue to work on group products this morning, switching to developing individual products this afternoon. Each of you will return to your agency with a draft plan for developing a needed partnership or enhancing the performance of an existing one.

SHOW OVERHEAD #1
MEMBERSHIP
RECRUITMENT
START-UP
MAINTENANCE
EVALUATION

Performance Objectives:

At the end of this training participants will be able to:

SHOW OVERHEAD #2
PERFORMANCE
OBJECTIVES . . .

1) identify stakeholders both internal and external to the organization

2) analyze the role of stakeholders in developing and maintaining partnerships

3) identify stakeholders that are potential partners

3) identify strategies for partnership startup, maintenance, and evaluation.

II INPUT

Step 3. Membership Recruitment (50 minutes)

CONTENT	TRAINERS NOTES

Depending on the model a wide range of members may be required.   The specific need and model dictates the membership of the partnership.

One of the best ways to identify partners is to identify the stakeholders of the potential partnership or program. Stakeholders are those person who have an investment or a special interest in the operation of the program.   Stakeholders can be positive or negative. It is important to identify the stakeholders, the nature of their stake and whether they are positive or negative. This will help you decide who may serve as a partner.
A typical list of categories of potential participants may look something like this:

Neighborhood association representative
Representative of neighborhood watch programs
Parent and youth group representatives
Local media representatives
Law enforcement representatives
City, County, State and Federal officials
School administrators, teachers, program providers
Religious leaders
Business leaders
Civic and service group representatives
Representatives of other non profit organizations
Labor leaders
Organizations or persons who provide specific services or have technical expertise

OVERHEAD # 3
POTENTIAL PARTNERS .

Methods of recruitment include:
    public announcement
    official appointment
    call for competitive applications
    recruit volunteers from specific organizations
    request specific organizations or persons to participate

ASK CLASS TO CITE EXAMPLES OF HOW PARTNERS/ PARTICIPANTS MAY BE RECRUITED. WRITE ANSWERS ON FLIP CHART.

Exercise: guided practice
The instructor should break the group into four small

LESSON PLAN: Planning and Developing Partnerships, Part 2

CONTENT	TRAINERS NOTES

groups.   Each group is assigned responsibility to identify the stakeholders of the specific partnership. Each group should be given the description of a problem and the type partnership to form. Group should identify the stakeholders, the nature of their stake (interest) and whether they are positive or negative stakeholders. A positive stakeholder would be supportive of the program, a negative stakeholder against the program. Of the stakeholders identified, the group should identify those they believe would make the best partners and explain why . Allow fifteen minutes in group and fifteen minutes to report. See below

DISTRIBUTE PARTNERSHIP DESCRIPTIONS AND ASSIGN ONE TO EACH GROUP.

FACILITATE REPORT OUTS.

    A. Advisors Committee for a substance abuse program in a jail.

    Problem: The program now ends when the inmate is released back to the community. No follow-up

    B. Citizens Group to guide the building of a new prison in a small rural community. The decision to build a new prison has been made and a small sales tax increase to finance it was approved.

    Problem: There has been some community resistance to the building of the prison from the city council.

    C. A task force to review the probation and parole classification system.

    Problem: There have been issues concerning the type (serious offender) and quality (lack of face to face contact) of supervision offenders are receiving.

    D. A network to coordinate client related information and services in a specific

LESSON PLAN: Planning and Developing Partnerships

CONTENT   TRAINERS NOTES

jurisdiction/community.

Problem: The county commissioners have demanded that client related services be better coordinated to prevent duplication and added expense.

Step 4. Start-up (50 Minutes)

Organizational meeting

The first meeting of the partnership should be used to establish guidelines, identify roles and responsibilities, provide structure.

OVERHEAD # 4
SUGGESTED AGENDA
ITEMS. . .

Agenda Items may include:

Describe needs assessment process and outcomes
Introduce members and rationale for recruitment
Discuss group goals and objectives
Clarify rules and responsibilities of members
Determine meeting and communication protocol
Set meeting/communication schedule
Establish policy and procedure requirements

BREAK INTO SMALL
GROUPS. FACILITATE
REPORT OUT.

Exercise: guided practice

In small group, the participants should develop an agenda for the first meeting of the partnerships identified in the previous exercise.   The meeting should last no more than two hours. Put suggested . agenda on flip chart paper. Allow fifteen minutes to develop agenda and fifteen minutes for report out.

Step 5. Partnership Maintenance (30 minutes)

LESSON PLAN: Planning and Developing Partnerships, Part 2

CONTENT	TRAINERS NOTES

Methods of supporting the partnership

OVERHEAD #5
METHODS. . .

      Training and education

      Assign responsibility for partnership maintenance/administrative support

      Maintain frequent communication telephone and written

      Coordinate meeting times and locations

      Form specific work subgroups

      Develop specific agendas and schedules

Ask participants to identify other area of responsibility they believe are necessary to sustaining the partnership.

      Step 6. Evaluation (50 minutes)

The evaluation process should be formative and summative.

Formative evaluation is constant. This process seeks to identify how the partnership is working.

OVERHEAD #6
FORMATIVE
EVALUATION. . .

      How efficient is it?
      How well are the partners communicating?
      Are partner needs being met?
      Is the partnership healthy?
      Are communications open and healthy?

Time must be set aside at every formal meeting of the members to discuss these issues. Discussions may result in changes in communication protocol, membership, procedures etc.

Summative evaluation is the periodic review and evaluation of how the partnership is achieving its goals

LESSON PLAN: Planning and Developing Partnerships, Part 2

CONTENT	TRAINERS NOTES

and objectives. This evaluation strategy requires measurable goals and objectives which can be reviewed on a regular basis, weekly, monthly, quarterly, annually. How often this evaluation needs to be conducted depends on the partnership's goals, objectives and longevity.

OVERHEAD # 7
SUMMATIVE
EVALUATION. . .

Quality Management

Any evaluation process must be grounded to the entire partnership process. The concept of Service/ Quality also referred to as Total Quality Management requires commitment from the very beginning of the partnership development process. There is a direct relationship between the partnership development process, previously described, and the quality/service plan. The elements of T.Q.M. are not just an evaluation strategy, but should be present in all the steps of the development process. Typical elements of a quality/service plan include:

OVERHEAD # 8
TOTAL QUALITY
MANAGEMENT

OVERHEAD #9-12
ELEMENTS OF T.Q.M. . .

Background - the reasons the organization is at this point, what has been done along these lines so far, and how this process will integrate with the past.

PRESENT EACH ELEMENT AND CONDUCT A BRIEF GROUP DISCUSSION OF EACH.

Theme - (if any is used) such as, "Service Excellence," Quality Has Value'" "Caring Through Service Excellence," "Quality is Job 1."

Definition of service/quality and improvement - how you are going to get everyone talking the same language and defining "it" the same way; how broad is your definition and scope of service/quality improvement.

Vision - a description of your preferred service/quality future concerning customers, employees, suppliers, systems and processes, shareholders, and industry leadership.

Values - the three or four core organizational principles

CONTENT	TRAINERS NOTES

that provide the behavioral context for this plan and all organizational activities.

Service/quality policy statement - this will be closely connected to your values. For example, XYZ means quality. Our dedication to quality has served us well in the past and is essential to our success in the future. Quality is not an option or a luxury; it is not the exclusive domain of selected departments or functional groups. Quality is everyone's job."

Implementation Schedule - the heart of the plan. This section is often very detailed and specific. It lists activities, primary responsibilities, objectives, and target dates to improve performance in each need. This schedule is usually shown in two stages; the first 12 months and the following 12-month period.

Training sub-plan - although this is part of the education and awareness, personnel, coaching, and training issues within the above implementation schedule, it is often extensive (and important) enough to warrant its own detailed plan.

Infrastructure - how facilitators, trainers, functional coordinators, local quality/service councils, line managers, and improvement teams work together. And how they link to the organization steering committee and strategic plan.

Assigned responsibilities - the responsibilities of the senior executive to front line supervisors, individual contributors, coordinators, and improvement teams, and the way in which everyone will be held accountable for improvement activities.

Resources and budget - the amount of money and time that will be devoted to the process, and the way it will be allocated.

The concept of T.Q.M. must be part of the partnership

CONTENT	TRAINERS NOTES

process from conception through retirement. It is not an evaluation strategy, but rather a process for striving for excellence.

(Jim Clemmer with Barry Sheehy and Achieve International, Zenger-Miller Associates, Firing On All Cylinders, ASQC, Quality Press, 1992)

III GUIDED PRACTICE

See II INPUT

IV CLOSE/SUMMARY

Given the last day and a half of instruction each of you should have a clear understanding and vision of what partnerships can mean to your agency. Given this information you will be given an opportunity to draft a plan developing or improving a partnership for your agency.

Following lunch each participating agency will have time to develop this plan and present it to the members of your small group for review and feedback. This experience is intended to allow you time and resources for applying what was learned in this workshop.

STAKEHOLDER EXERCISE

FOR YOUR ASSIGNED PARTNERSHIP IDENTIFY;

1) THE STAKEHOLDERS
2) NATURE OF THEIR STAKE
3) POSITIVE OR NEGATIVE
4) DETERMINE WHICH STAKEHOLDERS ARE POTENTIAL PARTNERS

PARTNERSHIPS

A. Advisors Committee for a substance abuse program in a jail.

Problem: The program now ends when the inmate is released back to the community. No follow-up

B. Citizens group to guide the building of a new prison in a small rural community. The decision to build a new prison has been made and a small sales tax increase to finance it was approved.

Problem: There has been some community resistance to the building of the prison from the city council.

C. A task force to review the probation and parole classification system.

Problem: There have been issues concerning the type (serious offender) and quality (lack of face to face contact) of supervision offenders are receiving.

D. A network to coordinate client related information and services in a specific jurisdiction/community.

Problem: The county commissioners have demanded that client related services be better coordinated to prevent duplication and added expense.

MEMBERSHIP RECRUITMENT
START-UP
MAINTENANCE
EVALUATION

Performance Objectives

At the end of this training participants
will be able to:

1) identify stakeholders both internal
and external to the organization

2) analyze the role of stakeholders
in developing and maintaining
partnerships.

3) identify stakeholders that are
potential partners

3) identify strategies for partnership
startup, maintenance, and
evaluation.

A typical list of categories of potential participants may look something like this:

Neighborhood association representative

Representative of neighborhood. watch programs

Parent and youth group representatives

Local media representatives

Law enforcement representatives

City, County, State and Federal officials

School administrators, teachers, program providers

Religious leaders

Business leaders

Civic and service group representatives

Representatives of other non profit organizations

Labor leaders

Organizations or persons who provide specific services or have technical expertise

Agenda Items may include:

Describe needs assessment process and outcomes

Introduce members and rationale for recruitment
Discuss group goals and objectives

Clarify rules and responsibilities of members

Determine meeting and communication protocol

Set meeting/communication schedule

Establish policy and procedure requirements

Methods of supporting the partnership

Training and education

Assign responsibility for partnership maintenance/administrative support

Maintain frequent communication telephone and written.

Coordinate meeting times and locations

Form specific work subgroups

Develop specific agendas and schedules

FORMATIVE   EVALUATION

SUMMATIVE EVALUATION

TOTAL QUALITY MANAGEMENT

Typical elements of a quality/service plan include:

Background - the reasons the   .
organization is at this point, what has
been done along these lines so far,
and how this process will integrate with
the past.

Theme - (if any is used) such as,
"Service Excellence," "Quality Has
Value"' "Caring Through Service
Excellence," "Quality is Job 1."

Definition of service/quality and
improvement - how you are going to
get everyone talking the same
language and defining "it" the same
way; how broad is your definition and
scope of service/quality improvement.

<u>Vision</u> - a description of your preferred service/quality future concerning customers, employees, suppliers, systems and processes, shareholders, and industry leadership.

<u>Values</u> - the three or four core organizational principles that provide the behavioral context for this plan and all organizational activities.

<u>Service/quality policy statement</u> - this will be closely connected to your values. For example, "XYZ" means quality. Our dedication to quality has served us well in the past and is essential to our success in the future. Quality is not an option or a luxury; it is not the exclusive domain of selected departments or functional groups. Quality is everyone's job."

Implementation Schedule - the heart of the plan. This section is-often very detailed and specific. It lists activities, primary responsibilities, objectives, and target dates to improve performance in each need. This schedule is usually shown in two stages; the first 12 months and the following 12-month period.

Training sub-plan - although this is part of the education and awareness; personnel, coaching, and training issues within the above implementation schedule, it is often extensive (and important) enough to warrant its own detailed plan.

Infrastructure - how facilitators, trainers, functional coordinators, local quality/service councils, line managers, and improvement teams work together. And how they link to the organization steering committee and strategic plan.

Assigned responsibilities - the responsibilities of the senior executive to front line supervisors, individual contributors, coordinators, and improvement teams, and the way in which everyone will be held accountable for improvement activities.

Resources and budget - the amount of money and time that will be devoted to the process, and the way it will be allocated.

NIC ACADEMY
LESSON PLAN COVER SHEET

Course Title: Building Partnerships " A Systems Approach"

Lesson Title: Correctional Partnership Workshop

Instructor(s) Experienced Correctional Trainers

Prepared by Vic Jacobsen   Date July 17, 1995

Time Frame

Total 3 hrs., 30 min.

Suggested Schedule:

Day: Two

Time(s):1:00 - 4.30 P.M.

Target Population: Correctional Staff

Number of Participants 24

Space Requirement Large room with two breakout rooms

Performance Objectives

Following participation in the workshop participants will be able to:

1) develop a written plan to develop a partnership upon returning to their home agency

2) present their plan to a small peer group and receive feedback.

Evaluation Procedures

(How will objectives be evaluated?)

Instructors evaluate the quality of the products developed by the participants and the quality of the surrounding discussions.